The
World's
Greatest
Collection
of
Fun Bible
Trivia

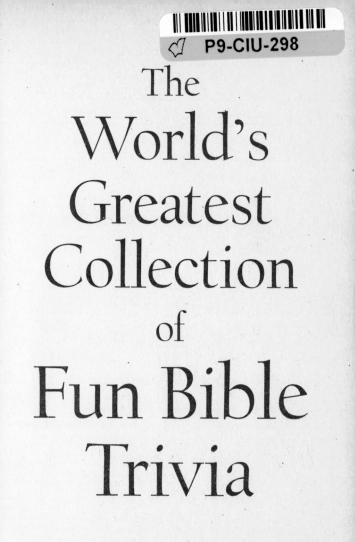

The
World's
Greatest
Collection
of
Fun Bible
Trivia

BARBOUR
PUBLISHING

Text is taken from *Fun Facts About the Bible You Never
Knew* by Robyn Martins, published by Barbour
Publishing, Inc.

Published by Barbour Publishing, Inc., P.O. Box 719,
Uhrichsville, Ohio 44683, www.barbourbooks.com

*Our mission is to publish and distribute inspirational products
offering exceptional value and biblical encouragement to the
masses.*

ecpa Member of the
Evangelical Christian
Publishers Association

Printed in the United States of America.

INTRODUCTION

Do you think you know everything there is to know about the Bible? Think again!

God's Word covers a lot of ground: more than five dozen books, nearly 1,200 chapters, more than 31,000 verses, and about 780,000 words.

This book is a collection of some of the most interesting facts and trivia of the Bible—you'll probably find many nuggets of information you never knew before! Each fact is followed by a scripture reference. Make sure to look up the facts that you find interesting, and you might learn even more!

Of course, knowing *about* the Bible and knowing the God who gave us His Word are two different things. As you read, keep in mind that the Bible is "quick, and powerful, and sharper than any two-edged sword, piercing even to the dividing asunder of soul and spirit, and of the joints and marrow, and is a discerner of the thoughts and intents of the heart" (Hebrews 4:12).

Don't just know the Bible—live it!

CONTENTS

ANGELS, PROPHETS,
AND PROPHECIES

Joel was a prophet whose name means
"Yahweh (Jehovah) is God."

—∞—

Children have angels in heaven who
always have an audience with God.
(Matthew 18:10)

—∞—

An angel started an earthquake by rolling
back the stone that sealed Jesus' tomb.
(Matthew 28:1–4)

—∞—

Prophets are men of God
who can tell the future.

The book of Psalms predicted hundreds
of years in advance that Jesus' hands
and feet would be pierced.
(Psalm 22:16)

—※—

An angel named Gabriel told Zacharias
his old wife would have a baby.
(Luke 1:13–19)

—※—

The first angels mentioned in the Bible
were holding flaming swords.
(Genesis 3:24)

—※—

Lucifer, Michael, and Gabriel were all angels.
(Isaiah 14:12; Jude 9; Luke 1:19)

—※—

The book of Daniel prophesies the exact years
of Jesus' ministry 600 years in advance.
(Daniel 9:24–26)

Centuries before scientists proved it,
Isaiah indicated that the world was round.
(Isaiah 40:22)

―⁓―

The prophet Jeremiah is described
in a variety of ways.
He has been called "the weeping prophet"
(Jeremiah 9:1; 13:17),
the "prophet of loneliness"
(Jeremiah 16:2),
and the "reluctant prophet"
(Jeremiah1:6).

―⁓―

The book of Micah prophesied Jesus'
birthplace as Bethlehem
700 years in advance.
(Micah 5:2)

―⁓―

The book of Psalms predicted Jesus' dying
words 1000 years ahead of time.
(Psalm 22:1)

An angel often came down to Bethesda
to stir up the waters of its pool.
(John 5:2–4)

—※—

Abraham is the first person in
the Bible to be called a prophet.
(Genesis 20:7)

—※—

The first vision mentioned in
the Bible came to Abram.
(Genesis 15:1)

—※—

There is nothing in the Bible
to suggest that angels were ever
human beings elevated to angelic status.
Rather, angels are spiritual beings
who were specially created by God.
(Hebrews 1:7)

Isaiah went around stripped and barefoot
for three years as a sign against Egypt.
(Isaiah 20:3)

—⁂—

According to Numbers, Moses was different
from other prophets because the Lord did
not speak to him in dreams, but face to face.
(Numbers 12:8)

—⁂—

In both the Old and New Testaments
the first accounts of visits
from angels are to women.
Hagar in the Old Testament
and Mary in the New Testament.

—⁂—

The first dream recorded in the Bible is that
of Abimelech which warned him that Sarah
and Abraham were really husband and wife.
(Genesis 20:3)

The only dream attributed to a woman in the
New Testament is the dream of Pilate's wife.
(Matthew 27:19)

—◊—

The prophet Ezekiel was commanded by
God to lie for 390 days upon his left side,
and then 40 days upon his right side.
(Ezekiel 4:4–6)

—◊—

Enoch is the first man recorded
as having prophesied.
(Jude 14)

—◊—

An angel of the Lord once called Ishmael
a "wild donkey of a man."
(Genesis 16:12)

Every three years Solomon's trading ships
returned home with gold, silver, ivory,
and a bunch of apes and baboons.
(1 Kings 10:22)

—⚜—

If a Hebrew person found a bird's nest
full of birds, he could take the babies but
had to leave the mother bird behind.
(Deuteronomy 22:7)

—⚜—

Animals have to answer to God, too.
(Genesis 9:5)

—⚜—

Moses had a staff that turned into a snake.
(Exodus 4:3–4)

God used hornets to drive enemy peoples
out of the Promised Land.
(Joshua 24:11–12)

—⁂—

Moses had a bronze serpent
that could heal snakebites.
(Numbers 21:6–9)

—⁂—

God once ordered ravens
to feed the prophet Elijah twice a day
while he was hiding in the Kerith Ravine.
(1 Kings 17:1–6)

—⁂—

God protected Daniel after he
was thrown into the lions' den
by sending an angel
to shut the lions' mouths.
(Daniel 6:22)

Adam named all the animals.
(Genesis 2:19)

—⟋⟍—

God made the first clothes for
Adam and Eve out of animal skins.
(Genesis 3:21)

—⟋⟍—

Jesus and Peter once paid taxes
with a coin found in a fish's mouth.
(Matthew 17:24–27)

—⟋⟍—

The raven is the first bird
mentioned by name in the Bible.
(Genesis 8:7)

—⟋⟍—

When Moses threw his staff
on the ground it turned into a snake,
and he ran away from it.
(Exodus 4:2–3)

Locusts are one of the most important
insects mentioned in the Bible,
making 56 appearances.

—∞—

Bears are rarely mentioned in the Bible
but they are used in visions that were
given to Isaiah (11:7), Daniel (8:5),
and John (Revelation 13:2)

—∞—

There are more references to sheep
in the Bible than to any other animal.
Sheep are mentioned over 400 times.

—∞—

Jacob gave at least 550 animals
to his brother as a peace offering.
(Genesis 32:13–18)

—∞—

Noah had only seven days to gather up
all the animals into the ark.
(Genesis 7:3–4)

Job once called himself a brother to
dragons and a companion to owls.
(Job 30:29)

—␣ৡ␣—

Among the different breeds
of sheep found in the Bible
there was at least one
which had a plump tail prized
for its fat (Exodus 29:22).
This large tail was fried and eaten.

—␣ৡ␣—

Laban is the first man recorded
as shearing his sheep.
(Genesis 31:19)

—␣ৡ␣—

God once provided a vine and made it grow
up over Jonah to give him shade.
But at dawn the next day
God provided a worm, which chewed
the vine so that it withered.
(Jonah 4:6–7)

The Egyptians did not like shepherds.
(Genesis 46:34)

—⚭—

John once saw three evil spirits
that looked like frogs.
(Revelation 16:13)

—⚭—

There is only one verse in the Bible
that refers to fishponds.
(Isaiah 19:10)

—⚭—

Although ferrets were around in the
Old Testament they are mentioned
only once in the Bible.
(Leviticus 11:30)

—⚭—

Flocks and herds were forbidden
to graze in front of Mount Sinai.
(Exodus 34:2–3)

Israelite spies who explored Canaan
said they looked like grasshoppers
compared to the giants they saw there.
(Numbers 13:33)

Samson set the tails of 300 foxes
on fire and set the poor animals loose
in some Philistine grain fields.
(Judges 15:4–5)

When Nineveh repented,
its residents even put sackcloth
on all their animals.
(Jonah 3:8)

Before an Israelite could offer
a ram as a burnt offering,
he had to wash its legs with water.
(Leviticus 1:9)

THE BIBLE

The shortest chapter in the Bible is Psalm 117.
It has two verses.

—⚌—

Psalm 119 is the longest chapter
in the Bible with 176 verses.

—⚌—

John wrote the book of Revelation
to seven churches in Asia.
(Revelation 1:4)

—⚌—

The Bible was written by more than
40 human authors inspired by the
Holy Spirit over a period of
about 14 to 18 centuries.

The Apostle Paul wrote 14 books
(over half) of the New Testament.

—◊◊◊—

In the entire book of Esther,
God is not mentioned once.

—◊◊◊—

There are nine Beatitudes found
in the book of Matthew.
(Matthew 5:3–12)

—◊◊◊—

There are only two books in the Bible
named after women,
Esther and Ruth.

—◊◊◊—

The Bible says it is better not to make
a promise than to break it.
(Ecclesiastes 5:5)

The book of Psalms has more chapters
than any other book of the Bible.

—⚏—

Paul wrote more books of the Bible
than any other man.

—⚏—

The first three words of both the book
of Genesis and the gospel of John are
"In the beginning."

—⚏—

The most comprehensive genealogical
list in the Bible is found in
1 Chronicles chapters 1–9.
It covers people from Adam to King Saul.

—⚏—

Every chapter of the book of Hebrews
either contains a quotation from the
Old Testament or mentions an
Old Testament character by name.

Solomon wrote two books
known for wisdom,
Ecclesiastes and Proverbs.

—⚍—

Moses wrote the first five books of the Bible.

—⚍—

David wrote the book of Psalms.

FOOD

Manna tasted like honey wafers.
(Exodus 16:31)

—⚌—

Israelites weren't allowed to eat camels.
(Leviticus 11:4)

—⚌—

God gave the Israelites quail
to eat before sending manna.
(Exodus 16:8–13)

—⚌—

When the Israelites first checked out Canaan,
they found grapevines so full it took
two men to carry a single cluster.
(Numbers 13:23)

If you stay awake, you'll have extra food.
(Proverbs 20:13)

—※—

After David brought the ark back
to Jerusalem, he gave a cake of raisins
and a cake of dates to each Israelite.
(1 Chronicles 16:3)

—※—

Israelites couldn't eat storks.
(Leviticus 11:19)

—※—

Once when Peter was really hungry,
he saw a sheet full of animals in a vision,
and God told him to eat up.
(Acts 10:10–13)

—※—

In Jeremiah's day, people put
scarecrows in melon patches.
(Jeremiah 10:5)

Israelites were not allowed to eat chameleons.
(Leviticus 11:29–30)

—ww—

John ate a scroll that was sweet as honey
but made his stomach sour.
(Revelation 10:10)

—ww—

People weren't given permission
to eat meat until after the flood.
(Genesis 9:3)

—ww—

Aaron had a staff that sprouted
blossoms and almonds.
(Number 17:8)

—ww—

Jacob traded bread and lentil soup
for Esau's birthright.
(Genesis 25:32–34)

Gideon once saw fire from a rock
burn bread and meat.
(Judges 6:21)

—∾—

Canaan is said to be flowing
with milk and honey.
(Exodus 3:8)

—∾—

Pharisees went to extreme lengths
to make sure that they never ate
anything that was unclean (Matthew 23:24).
They used to strain their drinking water
through a cloth to ensure
they didn't swallow a gnat.

—∾—

In New Testament times, washing one's hands
before a meal was the common practice
and was observed as a religious duty,
especially by the Pharisees.
(Mark 7:3)

The Israelites ate manna for 40 years
until they finally settled in Canaan.
(Exodus 16:35)

—⟋⟍—

After water, which was often impure,
wine was the most common drink
in Bible times.

—⟋⟍—

During the Passover, Israelites couldn't
break any of the bones in their feast,
not even the wishbone.
(Exodus 12:46)

—⟋⟍—

There is only one verse in the Bible
that speaks of onions.
(Numbers 11:5)

—⟋⟍—

The Bible refers to a frying pan twice,
and only in the Old Testament.
(Leviticus 2:7; 7:9)

Samson once brought a gift of honey
to his father and mother.
(Judges 14:8–9)

—w—

The first mention of cheese
in the Bible occurs in the story
of David and Goliath.
(1 Samuel 17:18)

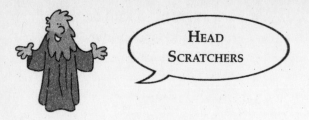

In ancient Israel, men closed
a deal by exchanging sandals.
(Ruth 4:7)

—⁓—

After Moses was given the
Ten Commandments, he wore a veil
over his face because he glowed.
(Exodus 34:33–35)

—⁓—

When Elizabeth was pregnant with John
the Baptist, Zachariah, his father,
was struck dumb until
the baby was born.
(Luke 1)

Once when Elisha prayed, God made
a whole band of enemy Arameans blind.
(2 Kings 6:18)

—⚬⚬⚬—

Job's wife thought he had bad breath.
(Job 19:17)

—⚬⚬⚬—

Once when Jesus was praying at the Mount of
Olives sweat fell from him like drops of blood.
(Luke 22:44)

—⚬⚬⚬—

The Ammonites tried to embarrass David's
men by shaving off half their beard and cutting
off their clothes at about mid-buttocks length.
(2 Samuel 10:4)

—⚬⚬⚬—

When Elisha learned that Jericho had
bad water, he made it better by tossing
in a bowl full of salt.
(2 Kings 2:21)

Once Ezekiel was sitting in his house
when a big hand picked him up
by the hair of his head and took him
somewhere between heaven and earth.
(Ezekiel 8:3)

—⟡—

When Moses led the Israelites out of Egypt,
he took Joseph's bones.
(Exodus 13:19)

—⟡—

Israelites were not allowed to have tattoos.
(Leviticus 19:28)

—⟡—

When King David was old he was always cold,
so he had a girl named Abishag
to keep him warm and wait on him.
(1 Kings 1:1–4)

Jonathan once killed a huge man
who had six fingers on each hand
and six toes on each foot.
(2 Samuel 21:20–21)

—⁓—

When King Belshazzar was drinking out
of a goblet from Jerusalem's temple,
a hand wrote a message on his wall.
(Daniel 5:3–5)

—⁓—

David pretended to be insane once
by marking up a door
and drooling all over his face.
(1 Samuel 21:13)

—⁓—

When Nebuchadnezzar went insane,
he grew claws like a bird,
feathers like an eagle,
and ate grass like a cow.
(Daniel 4:33)

The Philistines offered gold rats
as a guilt offering.
(1 Samuel 6:18)

—∾—

Once Jesus called demons out of a man
and sent them into a herd
of about 2,000 pigs.
(Mark 5:13)

—∾—

Aaron's hunchbacked descendants
couldn't offer food to God.
(Leviticus 21:20–21)

—∾—

A young man who had been following Jesus
ran away naked when his loincloth fell off.
(Mark 14:51–52)

—∾—

If you eat too much honey, you'll throw up.
(Proverbs 25:16)

When Cain was banished from Eden,
God put a mark on him
so no one would kill him.
(Genesis 4:15)

—✺—

Jeremiah wore a linen belt
that wasn't allowed to get wet.
(Jeremiah 13:1)

—✺—

When Aaron and his sons were ordained,
Moses had to put ram's blood on their
right ear lobes, right thumbs,
and right big toes.
(Exodus 29:20)

—✺—

Moses and Aaron gave the Egyptians
boils by throwing furnace dust into the air.
(Exodus 9:10)

Joshua made the Gibeonites
be woodcutters and water carriers
for the Israelites as a curse.
(Joshua 9:23)

—⟋⟍—

John the Baptist wore clothing
made of camel hair.
(Matthew 3:1–4)

—⟋⟍—

Two sounds made the walls of Jericho fall,
trumpets and a shout.
(Joshua 6:20)

—⟋⟍—

A man named Lot had a wife
who turned into a pillar of salt.
(Genesis 19:26)

—⟋⟍—

Samson lost all his strength
when someone cut his hair.
(Judges 16:19)

David won a wife by defeating Goliath.
(1 Samuel 17:25; 18:17–22)

—⦀—

Mary used her hair to wipe
perfume off Jesus' feet.
(John 12:3)

—⦀—

Jesus once cured a blind man
by spitting on his eyes.
(Mark 8:23)

—⦀—

Paul is stated to have had large handwriting.
(Galatians 1:1–4; 6:11)

—⦀—

Formerly in Israel, if a man went
to inquire of God, he would say,
"Come, let us go to the seer,"
because the prophet of today
used to be called a seer.
(1 Samuel 9:9)

God wrestled all night with Jacob
before changing his name to Israel.
(Genesis 32:24–28)

—◆—

Shadrach, Meshach, and Abednego
didn't even smell of smoke after being
thrown into the fiery furnace.
(Daniel 3:27)

—◆—

Three things were in the Ark of the Covenant:
the Ten Commandments,
a pot of manna, and Aaron's staff.
(Hebrew 9:4)

—◆—

Absalom cut his hair every year
when it got too heavy for him.
He would then weigh it and it typically
weighed about five pounds.
(2 Samuel 14:26)

Absalom once got caught in a tree by his hair.
(2 Samuel 18:9–10)

—⁂—

The one time that it is recorded
in the Bible that Jesus wrote,
he wrote on the ground.
(John 8:1–11)

—⁂—

Mark is the only gospel writer whose job
is not mentioned in the Bible.

—⁂—

King Nebuchadnezzar made his subjects bow
down every time they heard music.
(Daniel 3:13–15)

—⁂—

Samson had seven braids in his hair.
(Judges 16:19)

There are strange pillar formations
in the Southwest corner of the Dead Sea
known locally as "Lot's Wife."

—⚉—

Jews were instructed to make
a parapet around their roof.
They did this to make it safe so that
no one would fall off the roof and die
and make their family become
responsible for the death.
(Deuteronomy 22:8)

—⚉—

Ezra once stood on a wooden pulpit
and read the law of Moses aloud
from morning until midday.
(Nehemiah 8:1–4)

—⚉—

There is only one verse in the Bible
that mentions Easter.
(Acts 12:4)

When the Benjamites fought the Israelites
their army included 700 chosen soldiers
who were all left-handed, each of whom
could sling a stone at a hair and not miss.
(Judges 20:12–16)

—⟐—

Ecclesiastes tells us that riches cause insomnia.
(Ecclesiastes 5:12)

—⟐—

Solomon once sang of a woman
who had purple hair.
(Song of Solomon 7:5)

—⟐—

God once revived Samson with a drink
of water from the jawbone of a donkey.
(Judges 15:19)

—⟐—

The Israelites once built
an altar and named it Ed.
(Joshua 22:10, 34)

Job's friends once sat with him
for seven days and nights without speaking.
(Job 2:11–13)

—⋙—

Abimelech once told a story about
an olive tree, fig tree, and a vine
who asked a thorn bush
to be their king.
(Judges 9:8–15)

—⋙—

Samson once killed a thousand men
with a donkey's jawbone.
(Judges 15:16)

—⋙—

Joash was a young prince who was hidden
in the temple by his aunt for six years
to avoid the wrath of Queen Athaliah.
(2 Kings 11:2–3)

The prophet Balaam was once saved
from death by a talking donkey.
(Numbers 22:21–33)

—〰—

Solomon once killed a man
named Adonijah for asking
to marry his stepmother.
(1 Kings 2:13–25)

—〰—

King Jehoshaphat built a fleet of trading ships
that were wrecked before they ever set sail.
(1 Kings 22:48)

—〰—

Eglon, king of Moab,
was so fat that when Ehud stabbed him
with a one and a half foot long sword,
the handle sank into his belly.
(Judges 3:21–22)

When Asa, king of Judah,
was old, he got diseased feet.
(1 Kings 15:23)

—∞—

Jephthah and the Gileadites
guarded a spot of land
by asking Ephraimites to say
"Shibboleth." They were killed
if they couldn't say it correctly.
(Judges 12:5–6)

—∞—

During the whole time the Israelites
wandered around the desert,
they never got swollen feet.
(Deuteronomy 8:4)

—∞—

Zechariah saw a vision of a woman trapped
in a basket that was carried away
by two women with wings.
(Zechariah 5:6–9)

HOW MANY

The Levites had a mandatory
retirement age of 50 years.
(Numbers 8:25)

—⚬—

Ibzan, a judge, had 30 sons and 30 daughters.
(Judges 12:8–9)

—⚬—

The iron point on Goliath's spear alone
weighed about 15 pounds.
(1 Samuel 17:7)

—⚬—

It took 52 days to rebuild Jerusalem's wall.
(Nehemiah 6:15)

After the resurrection,
Jesus was on earth for 40 days.
(Acts 1:3)

—⟨⟩—

Moses was 40 years old when
he first visited the Israelites in Egypt.
(Acts 7:23)

—⟨⟩—

It took Solomon 13 years to build his palace.
It only took him seven years
to build the temple.
(1 Kings 6:38–7:1)

—⟨⟩—

Noah lived to be 950 years of age.
(Genesis 9:29)

—⟨⟩—

Noah was 600 years old
when God sent the flood.
(Genesis 7:6)

Saul, David, Solomon, and Joash
all reigned as kings for 40 years.

—∿—

When Jewish exiles left Persia
to build the temple in Jerusalem,
they took 30 gold dishes,
1,000 silver dishes, 29 silver pans,
30 gold bowls, and 410 silver bowls.
(Ezra 1:9–10)

—∿—

The new Jerusalem will be 1,400 miles long
and 1,400 miles wide.
(Revelation 21:16)

—∿—

King Josiah provided from his own livestock
30,000 sheep and goats and 3,000 cows
just for one Passover celebration.
(2 Chronicles 35:7)

Solomon wrote 3,000 proverbs
and 1,005 songs.
(1 Kings 4:32)

—∾—

Adam was 930 years old when he died.
(Genesis 5:5)

—∾—

David had 20 children.
(1 Chronicles 3:1–9)

—∾—

Solomon had 12,000 horses.
(1 Kings 10:26)

—∾—

Jacob had to work 14 years before
he finally got to marry Rachel.
(Genesis 29:20–28)

Moses spent 40 days and 40 nights on
Mt. Sinai getting the Ten Commandments
for the first time.
(Exodus 24:12–18)

—⟋⟋—

Pharaoh and the Egyptians suffered
10 plagues before Pharaoh agreed
to let the Israelites go.
(Exodus 1–12)

—⟋⟋—

The Bible says a strong man lives
to be 80 years old.
(Psalm 90:10)

—⟋⟋—

The Israelites marched around the city of
Jericho 13 times before the wall fell.
(Joshua 6:14–15)

After the great flood the water stayed
upon the earth for 150 days.
(Genesis 7:24)

—⚬—

Joseph was 110 years old when he died.
(Genesis 50:22)

—⚬—

The Bible says most men live to be 70.
(Psalm 90:10)

—⚬—

In the Bible children are named
28 times by their mothers and
18 times by their fathers.

—⚬—

There are 11 earthquakes
recorded in the New Testament.

The name "David" is mentioned
54 times in the New Testament.

—⚹—

Jabin king of Canaan had 900 iron chariots.
(Judges 4:1–3)

—⚹—

The Egyptians mourned the death
of Jacob for 70 days.
(Genesis 50:1–3)

—⚹—

Methuselah lived longer than anyone else
recorded in the Bible—969 years.
(Genesis 5:27)

—⚹—

Elijah once challenged 450 prophets of Baal
to see if their god would answer by fire.
(1 Kings 18:22–24)

The Philistine rulers each offered Delilah
1,100 shekels of silver for telling them
the secret of Samson's strength.
(Judges 16:5)

—⸙—

Shallum was a ruler of Israel
for only one month before he was
assassinated by his successor.
(2 Kings 15:13–14)

—⸙—

Samaria was built on a hill that was bought
for about 150 pounds of silver.
(1 Kings 16:24)

—⸙—

Gideon had 71 sons.
(Judges 8:30–31)

—⸙—

Jesus drove seven demons
from Mary Magdalene.
(Mark 16:9)

When the Israelites won the battle
with the Midianites, they got 675,000 sheep,
72,000 cattle, 61,000 donkeys,
and 32,000 "clean" women.
(Numbers 31:32–35)

—◇◇◇—

Noah's ark was three stories high.
(Genesis 6:15–16)

—◇◇◇—

Solomon's throne had six steps
and a gold footstool attached to it.
(2 Chronicles 9:18)

—◇◇◇—

King Amaziah had 10,000 of his enemies
killed by marching them off of a cliff.
(2 Chronicles 25:12)

THE FATHER
AND SON

When the Arameans were camped
outside Samaria, God made the sound
of chariots and horses and a big army
to scare them away.
(2 Kings 7:6–7)

—◊—

When God finally spoke to Job,
he spoke from out of a storm.
(Job 38:1; 40:6)

—◊—

Jesus chose 70 people to travel by twos
ahead of him and to heal people.
(Luke 10:1–9)

When Jesus returns, His angels will blow
trumpets to get everybody together.
(Matthew 24:31)

—⚮—

God once presented Himself to Elijah with a
whisper, preceded by a rock-shattering wind,
an earthquake, and a fire.
(1 Kings 19:11–12)

—⚮—

When Jesus died, saints rose from the dead
and walked around Jerusalem.
(Matthew 27:52–53)

—⚮—

God used dust to form the first man.
(Genesis 2:7)

—⚮—

God made the first woman
from one of Adam's ribs.
(Genesis 2:22)

Jesus was only 12 years old
when he amazed people in the temple
with His spiritual insights.
(Luke 2:41–52)

—⚬⚬⚬—

The name "Jesus" was chosen by God.
It means "the Lord saves."
(Matthew 1:20–21)

—⚬⚬⚬—

There are no stories about Jesus'
teenage years in the New Testament.

—⚬⚬⚬—

Jesus did not have a wife.
(Matthew 13:55–56)

—⚬⚬⚬—

Jesus was offered all the world's kingdoms
if he would worship Satan.
(Matthew 4:8–10)

Jesus said that only God the Father knows
the day and the hour of Jesus' return.
(Matthew 24:36–51)

—᙭—

God used a rainbow as a sign of
the covenant He made with Noah
and all living creatures
to never destroy the earth again.
(Genesis 8:21; 9:12–17)

—᙭—

Jesus was born about six months
after his cousin John the Baptist.
(Luke 1:36)

—᙭—

God once used a burning bush
to talk to Moses.
(Exodus 3:4)

Jesus said we could move mountains
if our faith is even as big as a mustard seed.
(Matthew 17:20)

—⁂—

God used a cloud to guide the Israelites
through the desert during the day.
(Exodus 13:21)

—⁂—

God made the sun, moon, and stars
on the fourth day of Creation.
(Genesis 1:16–19)

—⁂—

God was a whistler.
(Isaiah 5:26; 7:18)

—⁂—

God used a whirlwind to take
the prophet Elijah into heaven.
(2 Kings 2:1)

The first question in the Bible is
God's question to Adam,
"Where are you?"
(Genesis 3:9)

—⁂—

The name "Jesus" is mentioned
1,281 times in the Bible.

—⁂—

Jesus once saved the lives of his disciples
by stopping a storm.
(Matthew 8:23–27)

—⁂—

Thunder is frequently associated
with the voice of God in the Bible.
(Psalm 77:18; 104:7)

—⁂—

God created water
on the second day of creation.
(Genesis 1:6–8)

Lightning is frequently associated
with appearances of God in the Bible.
(Exodus 19:16; Ezekiel 1:13–14; Revelation 4:5)

—⁘—

Jesus is the only man in the Bible
described as using a towel.
(John 13:4–5)

—⁘—

The name of God appears
6,828 times in the Bible.

—⁘—

God used an earthquake to open the doors of
a prison where Paul and Silas were being held.
(Acts 16:25–26)

—⁘—

The Bible clearly states that the visit of the
Magi to Jesus was not on the night of his birth,
unlike the shepherds' visit to the manger,
but occurred later when Jesus was
staying in a house in Bethlehem.

Typical nativity scenes show several types
of animals around Jesus' crib.
The Bible doesn't mention any animals,
but simply says that Mary
"placed him in a manger, because
there was no room for them in the inn."
(Luke 2:7)

—⋙—

Shepherds did not typically spend
the night in the fields during winter.
This indicates that Jesus may have
been born in spring or summer.

—⋙—

The wise men, the Magi, were astrologers
and probably came from Persia
or southern Arabia.

—⋙—

Jesus was born in a cave,
not in a wooden stable.
Caves were used to keep animals in
because of the intense heat.

When Jesus was born,
Mary "wrapped him in cloths"
(Luke 2:7).
Jewish mothers believed
that if they wrapped up
their babies firmly in bandages,
then the baby's limbs would grow straight.

—∞—

The three gifts of the Magi had a
prophetic meaning: gold, the gift for a king;
incense, the gift for a priest; and myrrh,
a burial ointment as a gift
for one who would die.

—∞—

There are no references
to Christmas in the Bible.
The first Christmas celebration did not
occur until about 250 years after
the last book of the Bible was written.

The Bible does not say
how many wise men came to see Jesus.
The traditional number of three came about
because three gifts are mentioned.

—⁊⁊—

There is no New Testament record
of Christmas celebrations
and no date is given for the nativity.

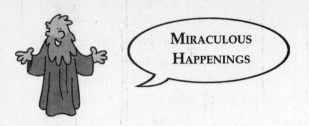

MIRACULOUS
HAPPENINGS

When Paul was building a fire,
a poisonous snake bit him on the hand.
People thought he was a god
when he didn't die.
(Acts 28:1–6)

—◊◊◊—

Once when Paul was speaking,
a man named Eutychus who was
sitting in a window fell asleep
and plunged three stories to the ground.
He died, but Paul prayed over him
and the Lord brought him back to life.
(Acts 20:9–12)

—◊◊◊—

God made the shadow on a sundial go
back ten steps as a sign to Hezekiah.
(2 Kings 20:11)

Moses hit a rock and got water when
he was just supposed to talk to it.
That's why he wasn't allowed
to move to Canaan.
(Numbers 20:6–13)

—⟐—

Once Jesus healed a mute man by spitting
and touching the guy's tongue.
(Mark 7:33)

—⟐—

People were healed just by
touching Jesus' clothes.
(Mark 6:56)

—⟐—

While some priests were carrying
the Ark of the Covenant,
the Jordan River dried up
so they could cross on dry ground.
(Joshua 3:15–17)

People used to lay sick people in the streets
so that Peter's shadow could heal them
as he walked by.
(Acts 5:15)

—⁓—

When the Egyptians were chasing
Moses and the Israelites,
God made the wheels fall off
of the Egyptians' chariots.
(Exodus 14:25)

—⁓—

When Jesus walked on water,
His disciples thought he was a ghost.
(Mark 6:49)

—⁓—

In His first recorded miracle,
Jesus changed water into wine.
(John 2:1–11)

After the Resurrection,
when Jesus told the disciples
to put their fishing nets
on the right side of the boat,
they caught 153 fish.
(John 21:1–11)

—◊—

Elijah divided the Jordan with his coat.
(2 Kings 2:8)

—◊—

With five loaves and two fishes Jesus fed
approximately 5,000 men.
(Matthew 14:15–21)

—◊—

Moses once threw a tree into
bitter water to make it sweet.
(Exodus 15:24–25)

Jesus' healing miracles were usually performed with a word of command. He had the kind of authority over disease that an officer has over subordinates. Twice Jesus "gave the order" without even seeing the patient.

—∞—

A man came back to life when his body touched the bones of the dead prophet Elisha. (2 Kings 13:21)

—∞—

A woman, who had been bleeding for 12 years, was healed by touching Jesus' clothing. (Matthew 9:20–22)

—∞—

Jesus once healed 10 lepers at one time. (Luke 17:11–19)

Peter performed his first miracle
after Jesus went to heaven.
(Acts 3:6–7)

—⚭—

Elijah was the first person to raise
someone from the dead.
(1 Kings 17:17–24)

—⚭—

God once made Moses' hand leprous
to show His power.
(Exodus 4:6–7)

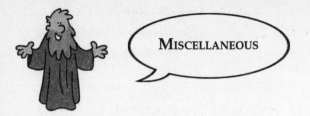

The term "scapegoat" comes from
the use of a goat that was to receive
the sins of the people and be
released into the wilderness.
(Leviticus 16:10)

—⟋⟍—

Onycha is an expensive incense
like musk that Moses used.
(Exodus 30:34)

—⟋⟍—

It didn't rain in the Garden of Eden.
Water came up from the ground
to make things grow.
(Genesis 2:5–6)

Crisping pins were purses.
(Isaiah 3:22)

—⚊—

Job was the first recorded person to say
"the skin of my teeth."
(Job 19:20)

—⚊—

Og, the king of Bashan, had an iron bed
13 feet long and 6 feet wide.
(Deuteronomy 3:11)

—⚊—

A withe is a strong twig (a thong in the NIV).
(Judges 16:7–9)

—⚊—

The Israelites wore tassels on their clothes
to remind them of God's commandments.
(Numbers 15:38)

Before a girl could be presented
to King Xerxes, she went through
12 months of beauty treatments.
(Esther 2:12)

—∞—

When Paul needed to escape from Damascus,
his friends lowered him from
the city wall in a basket.
(Acts 9:25)

—∞—

Once the people in
the synagogue in Nazareth
were so disgusted with Jesus
that they tried to throw him off of a cliff.
(Luke 4:29)

—∞—

Noah planted the first vineyard.
(Genesis 9:20)

Wisdom was made before the world began.
(Proverbs 8:23)

—⟨⟨⟩⟩—

Noah's ark was made of cypress wood
(gopher wood in the King James Version).
(Genesis 6:14)

—⟨⟨⟩⟩—

During the flood, water covered
the mountains by more than 20 feet.
(Genesis 7:20)

—⟨⟨⟩⟩—

Because the priestly garments were so sacred,
Hebrew priests had to take a bath
before they put them on.
(Leviticus 16:4)

—⟨⟨⟩⟩—

The hailstones that fell in
John's revealing vision
weighed about 100 pounds each.
(Revelation 16:21)

Kings went to war in the spring.
(2 Samuel 11:1)

—⚏—

The early church had a list of needy widows,
but you had to be over 60, a faithful wife,
and known for good deeds.
(1 Timothy 5:9–10)

—⚏—

Nothing in Solomon's house was made of
silver because it wasn't worth much then.
(1 Kings 10:21)

—⚏—

The Philistines kept Israel from having
blacksmiths because they were afraid
they would make weapons.
(1 Samuel 13:19)

—⚏—

The wave offering was called that because
the Israelites waved it at God.
(Exodus 29:24)

Once, David's mightiest men risked
their lives to get him some water from a well,
but David wouldn't drink it because of
all the trouble they went to.
(1 Chronicles 11:17–19)

—⚬—

David used a sword
to kill Goliath, not a stone.
(1 Samuel 17:51)

—⚬—

The reason for the first wind
recorded in the Bible was to clear
the flood water from the earth.
(Genesis 8:1)

—⚬—

God wrote the Ten Commandments
onto the stone tablets the first time,
but Moses wrote them the second time.
(Exodus 31:18; 34:27–28)

The ancient Israelites were to write
God's commands on their doorposts
as a daily reminder to themselves
and their children.
(Deuteronomy 11:18–20)

—⁘—

Noah and his sons were the first people
to ever see a rainbow.
(Genesis 9:8, 13)

—⁘—

Gideon built an altar he called
"The Lord is Peace."
(Judges 6:24)

—⁘—

When Paul and Barnabas
were speaking in Lystra,
they were mistaken for the gods
Hermes and Zeus by people in the crowd.
(Acts 14:12)

The disciples were first called
Christians in Antioch.
(Acts 11:26)

—⚬⚬—

Most of the plagues in Egypt
were brought on with a wooden staff.

—⚬⚬—

Three constellations that are recognized
today are mentioned in Job:
The Bear, Orion, and the Pleiades.
(Job 38)

—⚬⚬—

Other than the book of Genesis,
a rainbow is mentioned on only one other
occasion in the Old Testament.
(Ezekiel 1:28)

—⚬⚬—

The great flood officially started on the
seventeenth day of the second month.
(Genesis 7:11)

The "great and noble"
Asnapper was an Assyrian prince
who colonized the cities of Samaria after
the Israelites were taken captive to Assyria.
(Ezra 4:10)

—∞—

There are only two verses in the
New Testament that mention music.
(Luke 15:25; Ephesians 5:19)

—∞—

King Solomon had a throne
made out of ivory and gold.
(1 Kings 10:18)

—∞—

Amos is the only book in the Bible
to mention "a pair of shoes."
(Amos 2:6; 8:6)

There are two instances of
book burning in the Bible.
(Jeremiah 36:23–32; Acts 19:19)

—⟋⟋⟍—

The word "science" is mentioned
only twice in the Bible.
(Daniel 1:4; 1 Timothy 6:20)

—⟋⟋⟍—

The first record of a man shaving in the Bible
was when Joseph was brought before Pharaoh.
(Genesis 41:14)

—⟋⟋⟍—

God was responsible for the first wedding
recorded in the Bible.
(Genesis 2:18, 24)

—⟋⟋⟍—

The Ark of the Covenant and its carrying
poles were covered with gold.
(Exodus 25:10–14)

The covering for the tabernacle was made
out of ram skins and sea cow hides.
(Exodus 36:19)

—◊—

The Sabbath was measured from the evening
of one day to the evening of the next.
(Leviticus 23:32)

—◊—

Haman had a gallows built to hang Mordecai,
but he was hanged on it instead.
(Esther 7:9)

—◊—

The Sea of Galilee is also known
as the Lake of Gennesaret.
(Luke 5:1)

—◊—

Three o'clock in the afternoon
was prayer time in Paul's day.
(Acts 3:1)

Noah's son Shem was 98 years old
when the flood came.
(Genesis 11:10)

—⚍—

Judah had as many gods as they did towns.
(Jeremiah 11:13)

WHO AND WHERE

When King Xerxes couldn't sleep he had
people read the record of his reign to him.
(Esther 6:1)

—⚟—

Elijah outran Ahab's chariots
from Carmel all the way to Jezreel.
(1 Kings 18:46)

—⚟—

Luke was a medical doctor.
(Colossians 4:14)

—⚟—

Moses was three months old when
Pharaoh's daughter found him in a basket.
(Acts 7:20–21)

Goliath was over nine feet tall.
(1 Samuel 17:4)

—⚬—

Jubal was the father of people
who play harps and flutes.
(Genesis 4:21)

—⚬—

Abraham had two nephews
named Uz and Buz.
(Genesis 22:21)

—⚬—

Joash was only seven years old
when he became king.
(2 Chronicles 24:1)

—⚬—

Esau was sometimes called Edom,
which means red.
(Genesis 25:30)

Bethlehem means "house of bread."

—⁂—

Samuel's mother made him a little robe
every year while he was living with Eli.
(1 Samuel 2:19)

—⁂—

A man named Simon tried to pay
Peter and John for the power
to give people the Holy Spirit.
(Acts 8:18–19)

—⁂—

Every morning Job sacrificed a burnt offering
just in case one of his children had sinned.
(Job 1:5)

—⁂—

Jashobeam, Eleazar, and Shammah
were known as "the three."
They were David's mightiest men.
(1 Chronicles 11:11–12; 2 Samuel 23:11)

Only priests could carry
the Ark of the Covenant.
(1 Chronicles 15:2)

—⚏—

Some people, including Herod,
thought that Jesus was John the Baptist
raised from the dead.
(Mark 6:14)

Jericho was known as the City of Palms.
(Judges 1:16)

—⚏—

The Egyptians made slaves out of the Israelites
because they were afraid of them.
(Exodus 1:9–11)

—⚏—

Egyptians hated shepherds.
(Genesis 46:34)

Even before Jacob and Esau were born,
God told Rebekah that the older one
would serve the younger one.
(Genesis 25:23)

—⁂—

Noah was also used as a girl name.
(Joshua 17:3)

—⁂—

Abel was the world's first murder victim.
(Genesis 4:8)

—⁂—

Joseph was 30 when he became
a ruler of Egypt.
(Genesis 41:46)

—⁂—

In the new earth and heaven there isn't a sea.
(Revelation 21:1)

Joshua was the next Israelite
leader after Moses.
(Joshua 1:1–10)

—⁂—

God told Abraham that he would make his
descendants as numerous as the stars in the
sky and as the sand on the seashore.
(Genesis 22:15–17)

—⁂—

The disciple Thomas was later called
"doubting Thomas" because he couldn't
believe Jesus was risen from the dead.
(John 20:24–29)

—⁂—

Esau was the first redhead mentioned
in the Bible.
(Genesis 25:25)

—⁂—

Cain was the first child born in the Bible.
(Genesis 4:1)

Illyricum, a place Paul once mentioned,
is actually Albania and Yugoslavia.
(Romans 15:19)

—⚏—

Solomon was the wisest man,
next to Jesus, who ever lived.
(1 Kings 3:10–12)

—⚏—

Moses broke the tablets with the
Ten Commandments written on them.
(Exodus 32:19)

—⚏—

Esau and Jacob were two brothers
described as being "one hairy, one smooth."
(Genesis 27:11)

—⚏—

Samson once killed a lion
with his bare hands.
(Judges 14:5–6)

God used fire and brimstone
to destroy Sodom and Gomorrah.
(Genesis 19:24)

—◊◊◊—

Esther became queen by
winning a beauty contest.
(Esther 2:1–17)

—◊◊◊—

Nathanael was known as
"the Israelite of no guile."
(John 1:47)

—◊◊◊—

The longest name in the Bible
is Maher-Shalal-Hash-Baz.
(Isaiah 8:1)

—◊◊◊—

Enoch was the first city named in the Bible.
(Genesis 4:17)

Joseph, the husband of Mary, appears only in the narratives of Jesus' infancy and boyhood. This has led many to speculate that he had died before Jesus' public ministry began.

—⚉—

The name Moses is derived from the verb, "to draw out."

—⚉—

Naomi is the first person to be called a mother-in-law in the Bible.
(Ruth 1:14)

—⚉—

The Greek name Eutychus, belonging to the young man Paul raised from the dead, appropriately means "lucky."
(Acts 20:7–12)

—⚉—

Naamah is the first sister mentioned in the Bible.
(Genesis 4:22)

Saul and Og are two kings
who are described as extremely tall.
(1 Samuel 10:20–23; Deuteronomy 3:11)

—⚈—

Egypt was once ruled by a king named So.
(2 Kings 17:4)

—⚈—

There is only one verse in the Bible
that describes David as a psalmist.
(2 Samuel 23:1)

—⚈—

Paul was shipwrecked at least three times.
(2 Corinthians 11:25)

—⚈—

The only women described in the Bible
as kissing one another are Orpah
and her mother-in-law, Naomi.
(Ruth 1:14)

Only once in the Bible is the tabernacle
called the temple of the Lord.
(1 Samuel 3:3)

—◊—

Zacchaeus is the only man whom
the Bible describes as short.
(Luke 19:1–3)

—◊—

Sarah, Abraham's wife, is the first person
recorded to have laughed.
(Genesis 18:12)

—◊—

Rebekah is the first woman recorded
in the Bible as wearing a veil.
(Genesis 24:64–65)

—◊—

The young boy David played a harp
to soothe the troubled spirit of King Saul.
(1 Samuel 16:18–23)

Gideon was nicknamed "Jerub-Baal"
for tearing down Baal's altar.
(Judges 6:32)

—⚌—

Bezalel and Oholiab were
the two men chosen by God to
make the Ark of the Covenant.
(Exodus 36:1–2)

—⚌—

A man named Naaman once carried
home two loads of earth from Israel
after being healed of leprosy.
(2 Kings 5:13–17)

—⚌—

Cain was responsible for building the first city.
(Genesis 4:17)

—⚌—

Nahor, the name of Abraham's grandfather,
means "snorer."

When Joshua's army was taking over part of
Canaan, they crippled their enemy's horses
by clipping their hamstrings.
(Joshua 11:9)

—⚬—

Judah once had a ruling queen.
Queen Athaliah ruled for six years.
(2 Kings 11:3)

—⚬—

Jonah was inside the big fish
for three days and three nights.
(Jonah 1:17)

—⚬—

Esther's Hebrew name was Hadassah.
(Esther 2:7)